COLLECTION MANAGEMENT

SAMUEL HOUSTON

Military Heroes

SAMUEL HOUSTON

ARMY LEADER & HISTORIC POLITICIAN

by **Valerie Bodden**

Content Consultant:
Gregg Cantrell, PhD, Professor of History
Texas Christian University

ABDO
Publishing Company

CREDITS

Published by ABDO Publishing Company, 8000 West 78th Street, Edina, Minnesota 55439. Copyright © 2010 by Abdo Consulting Group, Inc. International copyrights reserved in all countries. No part of this book may be reproduced in any form without written permission from the publisher. The Essential Library™ is a trademark and logo of ABDO Publishing Company.

Printed in the United States of America,
North Mankato, Minnesota
102009
012010

 PRINTED ON RECYCLED PAPER

Editor: Chrös McDougall
Copy Editor: Paula Lewis
Interior Design and Production: Kazuko Collins
Cover Design: Kazuko Collins

Library of Congress Cataloging-in-Publication Data
Bodden, Valerie.
  Samuel Houston : Army leader & historic politician / Valerie
Bodden.
     p. cm. — (Military heroes)
  Includes bibliographical references and index.
  ISBN 978-1-60453-962-2
  1. Houston, Sam, 1793-1863—Juvenile literature. 2. Gover-
nors—Texas—Biography—Juvenile literature. 3. Legislators—
United States—Biography—Juvenile literature. 4. United States.
Congress. Senate—Biography—Juvenile literature. 5. Texas—His-
tory—To 1846—Juvenile literature. I. Title.

F390.H84B63 2010
976.4'04092--dc22
[B]
                                        ⟨B⟩
                                    J 976.404
                                        H 843
                                        2009032373

TABLE OF CONTENTS

A statue of Sam Houston leading his troops into battle is on display in Houston, Texas.

HERO OF SAN JACINTO

The afternoon of April 21, 1836, was clear and sunny. *A good day for a battle,* thought Sam Houston, commander of the Texas revolutionary army. Mounted on his magnificent white stallion, Houston looked at the line of soldiers stretched out in the thick stand of trees near the present-day city of Houston. There were 783 soldiers, most of them untrained militia. They were about to do battle with a Mexican force almost twice as large and much better trained. The battle was for the glory of Texas. The goal was to win independence from Mexico and avenge the Mexican slaying of hundreds of Texans at the fortresses of the Alamo and Goliad a month earlier. Since the massacre, Houston's men had been urging him to attack the Mexicans. Now was their chance.

Less than a mile away, across an open prairie, the Mexican army camped in another stand of trees. Mexican dictator Antonio López de Santa Anna led the Mexican army. Many soldiers, including the dictator, were napping. Others were building makeshift shelters or carrying water back to the camp. They had little fear that the Texans would attack today. But they were wrong.

Hidden within a stand of oaks, Houston formed his infantry into a long, thin line, two men deep. On one end of the line, 61 men on horses made up the cavalry. In the middle of the line, along with the mounted Houston, were two cannons, nicknamed the Twin Sisters. With everyone in formation,

Houston drew his sword and ordered the infantry line forward. The men advanced quickly and silently, crouching low in the tall prairie grass. Houston rode in front, ordering the soldiers to hold their fire.

When the artillery, which advanced ahead of the infantry, was within 200 yards (183 m) of the enemy camp, Houston gave orders to fire the cannons. Canister, grapeshot, and chopped-up horseshoes shot out. They blasted the Mexicans' fortification—a low wall made of baggage, packsaddles, and tree branches. Although the

Remember the Alamo

In San Antonio, Texan troops had strengthened a former Spanish mission, the Alamo, into a makeshift fortress. On February 23, 1836, Mexican troops initiated a siege of the Alamo. Although Houston had ordered the Alamo to be abandoned by Texan troops, approximately 240 to 260 Texans attempted to hold the fort at all costs. Eventually, as many as 4,000 Mexicans surrounded the fort. They waited more than a week before attacking on March 6. The Mexicans made it clear that they intended to kill everyone in the fortress. Although the Texans put up a strong fight, the Mexicans were true to their word. Bodies of 182 Texans were found at the site.

A little more than a week later, on March 19, Texan forces marching from the fortress of Goliad were captured by Mexican troops. Mexican dictator Antonio López de Santa Anna's orders were to take no prisoners. However, Mexican General José de Urrea marched the prisoners back to Goliad. A week later, on March 27, nearly all of the more than 400 Texans were shot. The two massacres fanned the flame of Texan hatred for the Mexicans and lit their desire for revenge, which they exacted at San Jacinto.

suddenly alert Mexicans fired in return on the Texans, Houston ordered his troops to hold their fire. He wanted them to be within point-blank range before they shot to ensure that they would hit their target. The Texan soldiers continued to advance until they were within 60 yards (55 m) of the tattered Mexican wall. Finally, on Houston's command, his soldiers took aim and fired. Black smoke from their guns filled the battlefield.

After the first volley, Houston ordered his men to reload. But, eager for blood, the men took up the cry "Remember the Alamo! Remember Goliad!" and charged the Mexican camp. Using their guns as clubs and pulling out huge Bowie knives, the men beat and stabbed their enemies to death.

In the midst of the chaos, Houston's horse was shot and fell to the ground. No sooner had he

A Tactical Trick

On the morning of April 21, 1836, Santa Anna received 500 reinforcements, bringing his total forces at San Jacinto to approximately 1,350. Still, this was only a fraction of the total Mexican troops in Texas. Not wanting his men to lose courage, Houston told them that Santa Anna had not actually received reinforcements but paraded the same men around his camp in order to intimidate the Texans. He told them "it was all a *ruse de guerre* [trick of war] that could be easily seen through—*a mere Mexican trick.*"[1]

mounted another horse than he felt a sharp pain above one of his ankles. A musket ball had torn through his boot and into his flesh. Ignoring the searing pain, Houston remained in his saddle to lead his men. However, just 18 minutes after the fighting had begun, the battle was already over. The Texans overran the Mexican camp, and the remaining Mexican soldiers retreated. The camp was surrounded on three sides by river, swamp, and bayou, so they had few places to flee.

Assured of victory, Houston tried to call his men back into line; he knew that Mexican reinforcements could arrive at any time, and he wanted his army to be prepared. The men, though, sought revenge for the Mexicans' earlier slaughters and continued to kill long after the battle had ended. Many Mexicans who had surrendered were shot, beaten, or stabbed to death. Finally, Houston

Historic Battleground

A woman owned the land on which the Battle of San Jacinto took place. She demanded that Houston's army remove the dead bodies covering the ground. Houston replied, "Madam, your land will be famed in history as the classic spot upon which the glorious victory of San Jacinto was gained!"[2] Despite the woman's insistence, the bodies were left. Texans returning after the war encountered a field full of corpses.

*Santa Anna surrendered to General Sam Houston
after the Battle of San Jacinto.*

managed to restore some level of order, and the men
returned to camp. In spite of being outnumbered
nearly two-to-one, Houston lost only 9 men, and
fewer than 25 were injured. In return, his men had
killed 630 Mexican soldiers and taken another 730
as prisoners.

Victory in this battle, known as the Battle of
San Jacinto, proved to be complete when Houston's
forces captured Santa Anna the next day.

Cowhands dressed in historic costumes rode on horseback past the Alamo during a modern celebration of Fiesta San Jacinto.

The Mexican dictator signed an armistice agreeing to withdraw his forces from Texas. The Texas Revolution was over—Texas would become its own country.

An American and a Texan

Sam Houston was 43 years old when he led the Battle of San Jacinto. He had already made a name for himself in the United States. He had fought in the War of 1812 and served as a congressman and governor of Tennessee.

He now considered Texas his home, though, calling it "the finest portion of the Globe that has ever blessed my vision."[3] After the revolution, Houston's loyalty to Texas led him to be elected its president twice and to serve in its Congress. Later, when Texas became a U.S. state—due in large part to Houston's efforts—he represented it in the U.S. Senate for 13 years. He went on to become governor of Texas. In 1860, he lost his race to be the Union party's presidential candidate. With the American Civil War looming, Houston fought to keep the United States together and to keep his state in the Union. His unpopular stance led to his removal from the office of governor. Through it all, Houston never abandoned his loyalty to his

San Jacinto Day

Texans today are still proud of the victory at San Jacinto. Every April 21, Texas celebrates San Jacinto Day. People across the state fly Texan flags from their homes. An official reenactment of the battle is held at the San Jacinto Battleground State Historic Site on a Saturday close to April 21. A family festival that celebrates the history and culture of Texas is also held at the historic site.

A Polarizing Figure

During his lifetime, Houston was a deeply polarizing figure. At times, politics in Texas were discussed in terms of Houston's beliefs. People were not for or against specific issues; rather, they were pro-Houston or anti-Houston. Houston's fame remained after his death as well. Two years before he died, Houston said, "My life and history are public property, and it is the historian's privilege to record the good as well as the evil I have done."[5] Since his death in 1863, more than 60 biographies about Houston have been published.

adopted homeland. Shortly before his death, he promised his thoughts would be focused on the "happiness of these people; the welfare and glory of Texas."[4]

Sam Houston had lofty ambitions as a politician.

*The Shenandoah Valley provided beautiful natural surroundings
for Sam Houston to explore when he was young.*

STRIKING OUT EARLY

Sam Houston began life far from Texas
on the Timber Ridge plantation in the
Shenandoah Valley of Virginia. He was born on
March 2, 1793, the fifth of nine children born to
Samuel and Elizabeth Houston. The large family

lived comfortably in a large, two-story house and kept a few slaves who worked their farm. Sam's father had served in the Revolutionary War and was an inspector of frontier militias. Because of his job, Sam's father was often away from home, and the tasks of raising the family and running the plantation often fell to Sam's mother, Elizabeth.

As a boy, Sam was expected to help on the plantation. However, farming bored him. He spent much of his time exploring the nearby forests and fields. Sam did not enter school until the age of eight, and even then he only attended sporadically. Later in life, he wrote to his oldest son that he had gone to school for less than a year total during his childhood. Yet, Sam enjoyed reading the books in his father's rather large library. Among his favorites was the Greek classic the *Iliad*, which he read over and over again. He eventually committed large portions of that book to memory.

Sam's Roots

John Houston, Sam's great-grandfather, immigrated to America from Ireland—although he was originally from Scotland. He came in 1735 with his mother, his wife, and six of their seven children. The family lived in Pennsylvania for a time before moving to the Shenandoah Valley in Virginia, where he established a successful plantation. When John Houston died, his son Robert took over the plantation. Upon his death, his son Samuel (Sam's father) inherited the property that included a large two-story house fronted by white columns. Sam Houston was born in this home in 1793.

Moving to Tennessee

Samuel Houston Sr. had arranged to sell the family farm in Virginia and buy land in Maryville, Tennessee, where he had relatives. He had to pay off debts incurred through his military service and long absences from the farm. At the time militia officers had to pay their own expenses. But when Sam was approximately 13 years old, his father fell ill during an inspection trip and died. Sam's widowed mother decided to carry out her husband's plans. The house and plantation were sold. The family loaded featherbeds, books, pots and pans, tools, food, and other essential items into two wagons and set out for Tennessee where land was cheap. They traveled approximately 300 miles (485 km) in three weeks. They finally stopped on Baker's Creek, near the small settlement of Maryville, Tennessee, where Elizabeth had friends and relatives.

A Young Country

When Sam Houston was born, the United States was still a young nation, having declared its independence less than 20 years earlier. By 1793, 4 million people lived in the 15 states of the new country. Virginia was the most populous of these states with 748,308 residents. During the seventeenth century, much of the population of Virginia had remained near the Atlantic coast. By the 1720s and 1730s, however, settlers had pushed farther west. By the time Sam was born, nearly the entire state was populated.

The Houstons packed up and moved to Tennessee when Sam was about 13 years old.

Elizabeth purchased 419 acres (170 ha) of land, and her sons quickly erected a one-story log home. The family slowly established a farm on their property and worked together to run it. As in Virginia, Sam still had little interest in farming. He often disappeared into the forest, where he would remain for hours or days at a time. Sam also continued his habit of skipping school and reading the books he had brought along from his father's collection.

Because he was unwilling to help on the farm, Sam was sent to work at the Maryville general store, where Elizabeth had purchased a partial interest. Sam enjoyed his work at the store even less than farming. At the age of 16, he struck out on his own.

Great Warrior and Trading Path

When the Houstons left Virginia for Tennessee, they were not alone. Thousands of other immigrants had also struck out on the Great Warrior and Trading Path. It was part of a network of old trails that had been taken over by whites as a road system. They headed for Tennessee, Kentucky, and the Carolinas in search of cheap land. The journey was not easy. Rainfall often turned the road to muck, while in dry weather, the wagons kicked up clouds of suffocating dust. Travelers often had to ford streams as well.

Life among the Cherokees

Sam Houston headed southwest and eventually came to a Cherokee settlement nearly 90 miles (145 km) away on Hiwassee Island, near where the Hiwassee and Tennessee rivers meet. This was not Houston's first encounter with the Cherokees. His family's land was near the boundary of their nation, and he had met many Cherokees during his forest travels. Known as John Jolly by the whites, Oolooteka led the Cherokees on Hiwassee Island.

Known for their hospitality, the Cherokees had accepted many whites into their tribe. Many chiefs were of mixed white and Cherokee descent. They not only welcomed

*Sam Houston's Cherokee name, Colonneh, means "The Raven,"
which symbolizes good luck in their culture.*

Houston—Oolooteka adopted him. Houston was
given, or took for himself, the Cherokee name
Colonneh (sometimes spelled Kalanu), which means
"The Raven." The bird was a symbol of good luck to
the Cherokees and may also have been a symbol of
wandering. Houston quickly adapted to their ways.
He donned their clothes, learned their language,
and took part in their dances and games.

Only a few weeks after he had left home, Houston's brothers found him on Hiwassee Island and asked him to return home. Houston told them that he preferred life with the Cherokees. Still,

Houston did not completely avoid his family. Every few months, he traveled to Maryville for new clothes, gifts for his Cherokee friends, and money from his mother. Occasionally, he also took up work as a clerk at a nearby store to earn a little money before returning to his life with the Cherokees.

When he was 19, Houston decided to return to the white world in order to

Oolooteka and the Cherokees

Before the arrival of Europeans in North America, the Cherokees lived across much of the Southeast, including parts of Virginia, West Virginia, North Carolina, Tennessee, Kentucky, South Carolina, Georgia, and Alabama. The Cherokees fought against white settlement on their land for nearly 200 years. By the time Houston went to live with them, they were largely at peace with the white settlers. Whites referred to the Cherokees as one of the "Five Civilized Tribes." The Cherokees had adopted many of the ways of the whites around them and were the most assimilated of all American Indian tribes. Like the white planters of the South, many Cherokees had large plantations worked by African slaves. Others operated prosperous stores.

When Houston joined the Cherokees on Hiwassee Island, Oolooteka was the leader of a band of approximately 300 native tribe members. His friendliness toward the whites had earned him the nickname John Jolly, and he had moved to Hiwassee Island to get away from Cherokee factions less congenial toward white settlers. Houston looked up to Oolooteka as a father figure for much of his life.

earn money to pay off his debts, but his experience with the Cherokees had been deeply important to him. He always acknowledged its influence on his later life. Speaking of himself in the third person in his memoir—a habit he picked up from the Cherokees—he later said that his "early life among the Indians was . . . a necessary portion of that wonderful training that fitted him for his strange destiny."[1]

THE SCHOOL TEACHER

Looking for a way to pay off the more than $100 in debt that he had accrued during his time with the Cherokees, Houston decided to open a school near Maryville. Although he had little formal education, he knew how to read and write and could teach basic arithmetic, history, and geography. Houston charged eight dollars for attendance at the school—a steep price at the time. The tuition

Houston and His Mother

After leaving to live with the Cherokees, Houston occasionally returned to Maryville to see his family, but he later cut off almost all ties to them. He rarely wrote to his mother or older brothers and corresponded more frequently with favorite cousins. Yet in his memoir, he wrote that his mother was an "extraordinary woman" who was "gifted with intellectual and moral qualities."[2] Biographers have pointed out, however, that this memoir was written with a view toward running for the U.S. presidency. It was likely slanted to make Sam Houston appear to be a loyal family man.

could be paid one-third in cash, one-third in cotton cloth, and one-third in corn. In spite of the high enrollment fee, Houston soon had 20 students. At the same time, Houston tried to further his own education at Porter Academy, but he soon gave up. His interest in teaching did not last long, either. After six months, he left his job as a schoolteacher and set out for new adventures. ⌐

*Sam Houston taught in a one-room schoolhouse that might
have been similar to the one shown here.*

*In the War of 1812, Cherokee, Creek, and U.S. forces fought
against the British and their Creek allies.*

A YOUNG SOLDIER

In March 1813, at the age of 20, Sam
Houston joined the U.S. Army. At six
feet two inches (1.9 m) tall with a muscular build,
he quickly showed a talent for soldiering. Houston
initially reported to Lieutenant Colonel Thomas

Hart Benton. Benton later recalled that Houston was always "frank, generous, brave; ready to do, or to suffer, whatever the obligations of civil or military duty imposed; and always prompt to answer the call of honor, patriotism, and friendship."[1] In July, Houston was made an ensign. In December, he was promoted again, becoming a third lieutenant. Later, in 1814, he was promoted to second lieutenant.

GOING TO WAR

Less than a year before Houston joined the army, the United States had entered the War of 1812. The Americans and their Cherokee and Creek allies fought against the British and their Creek allies. By the time Houston entered the army, the war was being waged across much of the country. In February 1814, Houston's regiment was sent to Alabama to aid General Andrew Jackson in putting down a Creek uprising.

On March 26, 1814, Jackson led his troops to Horseshoe Bend on Alabama's Tallapoosa River. The next day, they cornered a band of hostile Creeks known as the Red Sticks because of the bright red war clubs they carried. Houston's regiment was commanded to charge the Creek barricade. Houston followed his commanding officer, Major Lemuel Montgomery, who was the first man over the wall.

Within moments, the major was dead. Houston continued over the barricade. Landing on the other side, he was wounded almost immediately as an arrow pierced his inner thigh. He remained on his feet as long as he could and fought until the battle moved away from him. He asked a fellow lieutenant to pull the arrow from his thigh. After some effort, the barbed weapon finally tore from the wound and

The War of 1812

The War of 1812 was the U.S. extension of a European war. Since 1793, France and Great Britain had been battling one another. Their conflict began to affect the United States when U.S. ships trading with France were seized by Britain and vice versa. In addition, the British forced a number of U.S. sailors into serving in the British navy. Americans also resented the fact that the British had not pulled back to the boundary lines established at the end of the Revolutionary War. These tensions led President James Madison to declare war on Great Britain on June 18, 1812.

The war was fought throughout much of the United States. In the north, U.S. forces tried, but failed, to take Canada, which was under British control at the time. In the southeast, the war pitted the Americans against the Creeks, who had allied themselves with the British. A number of Creeks and Cherokees also fought for the United States.

In December 1814, the Americans and Great Britain signed the Treaty of Ghent in present-day Belgium. Although the treaty officially ended the war, word did not reach the United States for almost two months. Andrew Jackson led the Battle of New Orleans in January 1815, winning a decisive U.S. victory and bringing an end to hostilities.

opened a huge, bleeding gash. With a cloth pressed firmly to his injury, Houston limped to the surgeon, who could do little more than fill the wound with rags.

While Houston was recovering, Jackson made his way among the injured troops. This may have been Houston's first opportunity to talk to the general. Later that day, Jackson called for volunteers to assault the approximately 100 remaining Red Sticks who had taken shelter in a ravine under the river bluffs. Although barely able to walk, Houston volunteered to lead the charge. As he approached the Red Sticks' stronghold, Houston was hit again. This time, two musket balls struck his right shoulder and upper arm at the same time. He was carried back to the surgeon, who removed the ball from his arm. Another doctor told the surgeon not to bother with Houston's shoulder, because he

Houston and Jackson

From the time he first met General Andrew Jackson at the Battle of Horseshoe Bend, Houston looked up to Jackson. Like Oolooteka, Jackson became a father figure to Houston, who often stayed at Jackson's Tennessee home, the Hermitage. Upon Jackson's death in 1845, Houston laid his head on the general's chest and cried.

General Andrew Jackson later became president in 1829.

would likely die by morning. The doctors moved on and worked on those patients they thought might survive. Houston later said that "it was the darkest night of his life."[2]

Despite the doctors' grim expectations, Houston did survive the night. The next morning, he was loaded onto a litter and dragged 60 miles (97 km) to Fort Williams. Later, with the musket ball still in his shoulder and causing unbearable pain, he was carried home to Maryville. He spent several weeks at his mother's house recovering from his wounds and a bout with measles.

In October 1814, Houston traveled to Washington DC, which the British army nearly had burned to the ground only months before. While in the capital, Houston worked briefly with the Army Quartermaster Department. There, he learned that he had been promoted to second lieutenant in May based on Jackson's reports of his bravery at the Battle of Horseshoe Bend. Houston returned to Maryville by March 1815. By this time, the War of 1812 had come to an end, but rather than being

Continued Pain

The wounds Houston received at the Battle of Horseshoe Bend plagued him for the rest of his life. Although the operations performed on his shoulder restored the use of his right arm, it was never as strong as it had been before the battle. For years to come, he dealt with painful bone chips. Even more than his arm wounds, Houston's thigh wound continued to bother him. The hole left by the arrow continued to ooze until his death.

American Indian Territories

As people of European heritage moved farther south and west during the early years of the nineteenth century, they began to covet the land of American Indian tribes. Soon, the U.S. government began an official policy of removing native tribes to lands west of the Mississippi. At first, such removals—such as the one advocated by Houston—were voluntary. In 1830, however, the United States, under President Andrew Jackson, passed the Indian Removal Act. This required all tribes east of the Mississippi River to be relocated to Indian Territory, in what is present-day Oklahoma. The native tribal nations that refused to cooperate were forced to leave.

relieved, Houston was worried. He wanted to remain with the army, but the end of the war meant that the government would scale back the size of its fighting force to prewar levels. Houston requested a commission in the regular army, which he received in large part because of Jackson.

In 1815 and 1816, Houston underwent surgery on his shoulder, first in New Orleans and then in New York. The musket ball was removed along with a number of bone chips. After his operations, Houston served for a time under General Jackson in Nashville. In March 1817, he was promoted to first lieutenant.

Indian Agent

In October 1817, at Jackson's encouragement, Houston was appointed to serve as a government Indian Agent to the Hiwassee Cherokees. Two years before, a number of Cherokee chiefs had signed a treaty agreeing to give up their land in Tennessee in return for new land west of the Mississippi River. Although these chiefs did not have the authority to speak for all of the Cherokees, the government now needed to convince the remainder of the Cherokees, including Oolooteka and his band, to move westward. Jackson knew of Houston's history with the Hiwassee Cherokees and thought he might be able to persuade them to move.

Houston was torn by his new role. It required loyalty to the U.S. government, which he knew was treating the native tribes poorly. Houston resolved to do the best he could for the Cherokees under the circumstances. Putting on the traditional Indian clothing, Houston set out for the Cherokee lands and arrived in late November. Once again, he was among the tribe. Houston knew the situation was unfair, but he sincerely believed that if they moved west, the government

A Political Enemy

In February 1818, Houston traveled with a Cherokee delegation to Washington DC to meet with President James Monroe and Secretary of War John C. Calhoun, who oversaw Indian affairs. Once again accustomed to living among the Cherokees, Houston donned a breechcloth, blanket, and feathers for his official meeting with the secretary of war. Calhoun was angered by Houston's appearance, but Houston replied that he dressed as the Cherokees did out of respect for them. Calhoun became one of the many political enemies Houston would make during his lifetime.

would provide them with good land. Oolooteka and his people agreed to move soon afterward. With new government blankets, gear, and muskets provided by Houston, they set out for new homes in the Arkansas Territory.

Despite Houston's success, in February 1818, government agents accused him of slave smuggling and selling alcohol to the native tribes. Although an investigation proved that he was innocent, Houston was humiliated by the charges. On March 1, he resigned from the army. That June, he also resigned from his post as Indian agent.

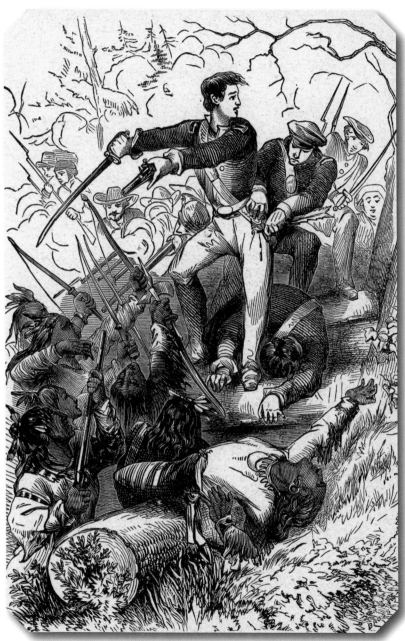

Houston led his troops against the Creeks during
the Battle of Horseshoe Bend on March 27, 1814.

Sam Houston's home in Washington DC

POLITICAL RISE AND FALL

After leaving the army and the Indian agency, Sam Houston looked for a new career. He decided on the law. At that time, law schools were beginning to be established on the East Coast, but most lawyers learned the profession by

serving as apprentices under practicing attorneys.
In the spring of 1818, Houston began to study law
under Judge James Trimble of Nashville, Tennessee.
Within 6 months, Houston had completed the
required reading—a task that normally took 18
months. By December, he had passed the Tennessee
bar exam that allowed him to practice law in that
state.

Houston quickly established his own law practice
in the nearby town of Lebanon, Tennessee. He
dealt mostly with minor civil and criminal cases.
His goal in becoming a lawyer was not necessarily
to practice law, however. Rather, he saw the law as
a stepping-stone to political office. In the fall of
1819, less than a year after opening his law office,
Houston campaigned for solicitor general (or
district attorney) of the Nashville district. Thanks
to Andrew Jackson's support, he was elected to the
office and moved to Nashville. The position did not
pay enough, however. After a year, Houston resigned
and began a private practice in Nashville.

Congressman Houston

In February 1823, Houston announced that
he would run for a seat in the U.S. House of

Representatives. In September, he was elected and soon headed for Washington DC. In Congress, Houston sat on the Military Affairs Committee, which oversaw the U.S. War Department. He cast votes in favor of numerous projects to bring improvements to western states such as Tennessee.

Dressed to Impress

In order to gather votes in the Tennessee race for governor, Houston rode to polling stations across Nashville on Election Day 1827. He made quite an impression on voters with his ruffled shirt, black satin waistcoat, native tribal hunting shirt, beaded sash, and embroidered silk socks. A black beaver hat completed the look. Apparently, the tactic worked—Houston won.

In addition, he drafted campaign materials for his mentor, Andrew Jackson, who was running in the 1824 presidential election.

Although Jackson lost his election, Houston was easily reelected when his term was up. By 1827, he was ready for a new political office and ran for governor of Tennessee. On Election Day in August, Houston easily won the race. As governor, Houston continued to focus on bringing improvements to his state, such as a canal to aid navigation on the Tennessee River. Houston was a popular governor, and after Jackson was elected president in 1828, many assumed that Houston would eventually succeed him.

Mr. and Mrs. Houston

For many years, Houston had joked that he could not marry until he made his fortune. After becoming governor, he decided that he was ready to take a wife. On January 22, 1829, 35-year-old Houston married 19-year-old Eliza Allen, a young Tennessee beauty from a powerful and ambitious family. Houston and his new wife returned to Nashville and settled at the Nashville Inn.

Just days after the wedding, Houston announced that he would run for reelection. In April, he was scheduled to debate his opponent in a nearby town. When he returned home from the successful evening, he discovered that his wife had left. Houston refused to speak of the separation throughout his life, and it has become the cause of much debate over the years. According to Houston biographer James Haley, Eliza most likely left because she was in love with someone else. Haley suggests that Eliza had been forced to marry Houston by her parents, who wanted to advance the family's standing in society.

As rumors of the separation flew across Nashville, Houston shied away from company. He kept to himself in his rooms at the Nashville Inn with only a few close friends. Many residents of Tennessee believed that Houston had wronged Eliza after hearing statements made by the Allen family, and angry mobs formed in Nashville. Some residents hung Houston in effigy. Friends urged Houston to speak out about the scandal and clear his name, but Houston refused. He later said that he told them:

This is a painful, but it is a private affair. I do not recognize the right of the public to interfere in it, and I shall treat the public just as though it had never happened. . . . It is no part of the conduct of a gallant or a generous man to take up arms against a woman.[1]

With his reputation shattered and his heart sorely wounded, Houston stepped down as

Why Did Eliza Leave?

Over the years, a number of theories have been put forth as to why Eliza left Houston only months after the two were married. Some historians have speculated that Houston accused Eliza of cheating or that Eliza was repulsed by Houston's war injuries.

Before she died, Eliza offered her own version of events to a friend. She stated that Houston had been an extremely jealous husband. He had locked her in a room at her aunt's house when he was gone so that she would not be able to talk to anyone else. Houston biographer James Haley asserts that there are many holes in Eliza's story. He claims that Houston never showed jealousy in any of his other relationships and that there is no indication that the couple ever stayed with one of Eliza's aunts. He also points out that on the second day of the marriage, Eliza told an acquaintance that she wished her new husband were dead.

governor of Tennessee on April 16,
1829.

BACK TO THE CHEROKEES

The next week, Houston boarded
a riverboat on the Cumberland
River. He headed for Arkansas
Territory, where Oolooteka and his
people were now living. Houston
arrived in late spring and was greeted
with a warm embrace from his old
friend. He easily fell back into life
with the Cherokees. Once again, he
donned native clothing and spoke the
Cherokee language—some even said
he went so far as to refuse to speak English.

Because the native tribes of the area knew
of Houston's influence with Jackson, they were
soon approaching him to intervene with the
U.S. government on their behalf. Not only the
Cherokees, but also the Osages, the Creeks, the
Choctaws, and the Pawnees sought Houston's help.
Houston negotiated a number of treaties between
the tribes and sent letters to Washington DC on their
behalf. In recognition of his position within their

Speaking Out

While living with the
Cherokees in Arkansas
Territory, Houston wrote
a series of articles in
defense of their rights,
though doing so was an
unpopular move at the
time. In one article he
wrote, "Where stood the
Indian of other days? He
stood on the shore of the
Atlantic, and beheld, each
morning, the sun roll-
ing from the bosom of its
green waves. . . . That age
has long gone by. . . . A
succession of injuries has
broken his proud spirit."[2]

*Sam Houston dressed as a Cherokee chief during
his time in Arkansas Territory.*

tribe, the Cherokees granted Houston citizenship
in October 1829. That December, the Cherokees
sent their new citizen, along with a delegation of
tribespeople, to Washington DC to negotiate with
the government on issues such as the expansion of
their lands.

A New Wife

Soon after Houston returned to Arkansas
Territory, he married Diana Rogers Gentry, a
mixed-blood Cherokee. The two set up a home and

trading post called Wigwam Neosho. For many years, Houston had been a hard drinker and now he was drinking even more heavily. Houston often visited Cantonment Gibson, the nearby army outpost, where he sometimes became so inebriated that his wife had to throw him over his horse to get him home.

Houston's drinking soon began to affect his relationship with the Cherokees, some of whom nicknamed him *Oo-tse-tee Ar-dee-tah-skee*, or "Big Drunk." When he ran for a position on the Cherokee Council, he lost.

Reentering Politics

Although hurt by the Cherokees' rejection of his bid for the council, Houston again agreed to represent them in Washington DC in early 1832. While there, Houston learned that Congressman William Stanbery had spoken harsh words about him. Stanbery had said on the floor of the U.S. House of Representatives that Houston had illegally attempted to obtain a contract for rations for American Indian tribes. Angered by the remark, Houston sent a note to Stanbery. Fearing a duel, Stanbery refused to read it. On April 13, Houston spotted Stanbery outside.

He approached the congressman and began to beat him over the head with his cane. Trying to fend off the blows, Stanbery pulled a pistol, but it misfired.

Four days later, the U.S. House of Representatives voted to arrest Houston. Not only had he beaten a congressman, but he had done so for words spoken on the floor of the House, which were supposed to be privileged. Houston was tried before the House with Francis Scott Key—author of "The Star-Spangled Banner"—as his defense attorney.

The trial lasted nearly a month. Finally, on May 7, Houston delivered his own closing argument. He did not deny the attack but questioned the principle of congressional privilege and the right of a member of Congress to publicly defame a private citizen. Although Houston's speech was met with applause from those who had gathered to watch the trial, he lost the case. Despite his punishment, the scandal ended to Houston's benefit by bringing him back into the national limelight. As he later said:

> *I was dying out, and had they taken me before a Justice of the Peace and fined me ten dollars for assault and battery, they would have killed me. But they gave me a national tribunal for a theatre, and that set me up again.* [3]

An image of Sam Houston circa 1826. Houston moved to Washington DC in 1832 to represent the Cherokees.

Much of Texas, the Southwest, and the West belonged to Mexico before the land became several U.S. states.

COMMANDER IN CHIEF

While in Washington DC, Sam Houston had begun to form a plan for another new adventure: a move to Texas. Although Texas was part of Mexico at the time, the United States had been interested in acquiring the huge area for many years. Since President Jackson's first year in office, he had been attempting to purchase Texas from Mexico, but Mexico refused to sell. A number of American filibusters, or men acting on their own initiative, had also tried at various times to take Texas by force, but they all had failed. Rumors had spread for years that Houston intended to enter Texas as a filibuster someday. However, political enemies spread most of these rumors.

In 1832, Jackson decided to send Houston to Texas as an Indian agent. Houston began his journey by returning to Wigwam Neosho. From there, he left Diana—giving her the trading post and nearly all of their possessions—and headed for the Texas border on a worn old horse. There, Houston met with the Comanche tribe to arrange a peace with the American Indian groups that were being relocated to the Indian Territory just north of the Texas border.

LIFE IN TEXAS

On December 2, 1832, Houston crossed the Red River into Texas. He acquired a tract of land and quickly set about completing his business by inviting the Comanche tribe to a meeting. He then began to study the political climate of his new homeland.

Houston sensed that changes were coming to Texas, as the settlers—most of them American—resented many of the laws the Mexicans had imposed on them. In 1824, the Mexican government combined the sparsely populated Texas with Coahuila to the south. This gave Texas, with a much smaller population than Coahuila, little say in running its own affairs. An 1830 law banning further immigration of Americans into Texas further angered the settlers, although the law had little effect, and the number of immigrants actually increased. Threats to enforce an

Early Texas History

Before the arrival of Europeans, Texas was populated by a number of American Indian tribes, including the Coahuiltecans, the Karankawas, the Caddos, the Jumanos, and the Apaches. The first Europeans in Texas were Spanish explorers who arrived in the early sixteenth century. Although Spain, which ruled Mexico at the time, claimed the land, it did not begin to establish missions there until the late seventeenth century. By the early nineteenth century, Texas was still sparsely populated with only three settlements: San Antonio, Goliad, and Nacogdoches.

In 1821, Mexico won independence from Spain. That same year, American Stephen Austin founded his colony in Texas. Austin had been granted a huge tract of land in return for bringing at least 300 families into Texas. These new settlers, in turn, received free land. Soon, this system, known as the *empresario* system, attracted thousands of settlers. Others arrived outside the empresario system by simply staking their own claims to the vast landscape. When Houston arrived in 1832, more than 15,000 U.S. settlers lived in Texas.

antislavery law also enraged many colonists, some of whom had set up vast plantations in Texas.

Houston settled in the town of Nacogdoches. In 1833, he was elected to serve as one of the town's delegates to a convention being held in San Felipe. The group was to discuss how best to seek Texas statehood separate from Coahuila. Some delegates called for Texas to immediately declare its independence from Mexico. But Houston sided with those who wanted to remain a part of Mexico as a separate state. He also called for Mexico to again allow immigration from the United States. Immigration was eventually made legal again, although the appeal for separate statehood was denied.

Soon after the convention, Houston returned to the United States to seek treatment for his shoulder wound. He spent much of 1834 there. Although the purpose of his long trip remains a matter of speculation, some biographers believe he was there to make plans relating to the future of Texas.

Volunteers Needed

Immediately after the first shots were fired in the Texas Revolution, Houston sent word to the United States requesting volunteers to join the fight. Men from a number of states, including Georgia, Alabama, Kentucky, and Louisiana, came to help. In addition, people in the city of Cincinnati, Ohio, sent the two cannons—the Twin Sisters—that the Texan army used to win the Battle of San Jacinto.

Sam Houston was busy working as a lawyer in 1836.

PREPARING FOR REVOLUTION

When Houston returned to Texas at the end of 1834, he dedicated himself to the law practice he had established in Nacogdoches. Throughout the beginning months of 1835, Houston remained a busy lawyer, defending both Texans and Spanish-speaking residents of Texas. He also prepared for the revolution that he sensed was looming.

He was right. On October 2, 1835, Texans in the city of Gonzales fired their cannons on Mexican

forces near the city. The Texas
Revolution had begun. Less than
a week later, Houston was selected
to lead the volunteer troops of
Nacogdoches. He gathered his men
and rallied them to the fight:

> *War in defense of our rights must be our
> motto! . . . The morning of glory has
> dawned upon us. The work of Liberty has
> begun. Our actions are to become a part
> of the history of mankind.*[1]

In November, with the support of
Houston and most other Anglos, or
white Texans, representatives met in
San Felipe. Houston and the majority
of other delegates favored seeking
Mexican statehood. A provisional
government was set up, and Houston
was appointed major general of the
Texas army. Houston soon found,
however, that his army did not exist yet. He was not
given command of volunteers, and most of the men
under arms in Texas were volunteers. Essentially, he
was a general without an army.

Antonio López de Santa Anna

Antonio López de Santa Anna was a key figure in Mexico for more than a quarter of a century. In 1821, he supported revolutionary leader Agustín de Iturbide in the war for Mexican independence from Spain. Two years later, Santa Anna helped to overthrow Iturbide and establish a republic. In 1833, he was elected president of Mexico. Two years later, he established himself as dictator. Although forced to retire after his defeat in the Texas Revolution, Santa Anna again rose to power and ruled Mexico from 1841 to 1845, 1846 to 1848, and 1853 to 1855.

In late February 1836, while the new Texas state government was proving ineffectual and Mexican forces under dictator Santa Anna prepared to march across Texas, another convention was called. This time, Houston and the majority of the delegates were in favor of declaring independence. On March 2, 1836, the convention signed a declaration of independence, proclaiming that they were now free from Mexican rule. Houston was appointed commander in chief of all Texas forces.

The "Runaway Scrape"

On March 6, Mexican troops slaughtered 182 Texans trapped in the fortress of the Alamo in San Antonio. Believing that the Mexican army might have as many as 10,000 troops in Texas (the actual number was closer to 6,000), Houston organized his 374 men for retreat. Weeks later, while Houston's men were still retreating, nearly 400 Texans were killed at the fortress known as Goliad. Even after Goliad, Houston pushed on with the retreat. Many of his men were angered by Houston's order to retreat, but the commander in chief thought it was the most prudent course of action:

We could have met the enemy, and avenged some of our wrongs; but, detached as we were, without supplies for the men in camp, . . . it would have been madness to hazard a contest. [2]

Although many of his men believed Houston's decision reflected cowardice, his plan was to build up the strength and fighting capability of his army before facing the enemy. For more than a month, Houston and his men retreated. In late March, they crossed the Colorado River, using it as a barrier between themselves and the approaching Mexicans from the south.

Meanwhile, Houston's army had grown in size as new volunteers from both Texas and the United States met up with the force. As the men marched north, families of Texans joined them. After the horrors at the Alamo and Goliad, even ordinary citizens feared for their lives, and they became refugees. However, as the retreat continued, a number of soldiers left in protest. David Burnet,

Mixed Opinions

Feelings about Houston within the Texas army varied dramatically. Many officers viewed him as a coward for ordering retreat. For years after the war, they made vicious accusations against their former general. Many more men respected Houston and his dedication to his soldiers. During the long retreat, many were impressed that Houston joined them in pushing the cannons and wagons through the mud. They placed their complete confidence in his ability to lead them to victory.

the temporary president of Texas, also was angered by the retreat. Houston, however, continued to fall back. His retreat, along with the civilian refugee movement, became known as the "Runaway Scrape."

Victory at Last

In April, Houston got a break. He learned that Santa Anna, with a smaller force of several hundred men, was headed for Harrisburg. Houston pushed his troops toward the village, marching 55 miles (89 km) in less than three days. When they arrived, they found the village in ruins. They continued their march, crossing Buffalo Bayou and setting up camp near the San Jacinto River on April 20.

Santa Anna's army arrived shortly after the Texans. Although the armies engaged almost immediately, Santa Anna withdrew his force after a brief artillery duel followed by a cavalry skirmish. Although Houston's men wanted to pursue the battle, Houston called them off. The next day, however, he led a surprise attack on the Mexican troops. In less than 20 minutes, they were victorious in the Battle of San Jacinto. The following day, Santa Anna was captured, and the Mexican dictator agreed to withdraw his troops. The revolution was over.

General Sam Houston rode on horseback at San Jacinto.

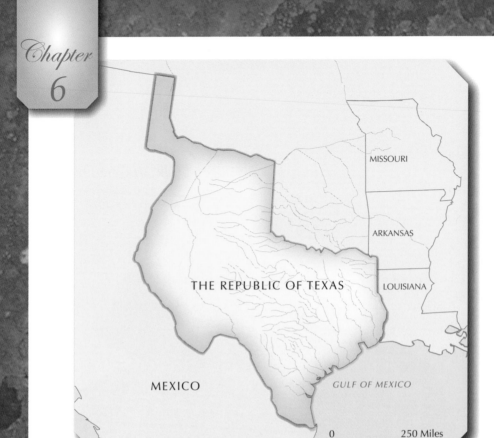

The Republic of Texas in 1836

PRESIDENT OF
THE REPUBLIC

lthough Sam Houston had led his men to victory in the Battle of San Jacinto, he had not escaped unharmed. A musket ball shattered one of his ankles. By the beginning of May, the wound was becoming dangerously infected.

He sought treatment in New Orleans. On his arrival, Houston was greeted by a large, adoring crowd. He tried to greet his admirers but was too weak, and he fainted from the effort.

Physicians soon worked on Houston's mangled leg. They cut away rotting skin and pulled bone fragments from the wound. After the operation, Houston spent several months recovering. By August, he was strong enough to return to Texas.

The President

Now that Texas was an independent nation, it needed a president. Initially, only Stephen Austin and Henry Smith declared that they would run for the office. Houston felt concerned that the candidates were too divisive. Knowing that Texas needed someone to unify its people, Houston declared that he, too, would run. Though he did so only 11 days before the election, Houston won in a landslide victory with 80 percent of the vote.

As he entered his new office, Houston faced a number of pressing issues. Despite the peace treaty between Texas and Mexico, the Mexican government had not yet recognized independence for Texas. That meant Texas constantly faced the fear that Mexico would invade again. Rumors that Mexican forces had entered Texas continually circulated.

Houston's Home

Even as president of Texas, Houston lived in a crude wooden shack. In 1837, American naturalist John James Audubon visited Houston at his home. He wrote that Houston's house was small and very dirty, and it had only two rooms and a dirt floor. Houston did not even have the small, two-room cabin to himself. He had invited physician Ashbel Smith to share it with him. Still, Houston rarely complained about his living situation.

With no money in the treasury, the Texan army was poorly supplied and running out of food. Attempting to provide for his forces, Houston sent a letter to New Orleans. He begged the commissary general to send weapons, shirts, shoes, and other supplies. The Texas president pledged his own land as security for any debts incurred.

Houston also attempted to restore relations with the Cherokees. They were angry that the Texas Congress had refused to sign an earlier treaty granting them land rights. With the Mexicans urging the Cherokees to attack Texas, Houston worried that the Cherokees might resort to war. He continually corresponded with tribal leaders and managed to maintain a tense peace with the Cherokees throughout most of his term.

A New Direction

During the election of September 1836, Texan voters had not only elected a president; they had also cast their votes in favor of a new direction for their young country. They were clearly in favor of annexation, or becoming part of the United States. More than 5,000 ballots were cast, and as few as 94 voters opposed the idea. Annexation was not up to the people of Texas alone, however. The United States had to agree to make Texas part of its union.

Although most Texans, including Houston, assumed that the United States would be eager to annex new territory, they soon found that they were mistaken. The American government worried that acquiring Texas might spark a war with Mexico. In addition, tensions between the southern slave states and northern antislavery states were beginning to escalate. Bringing Texas into the

Anniversary Celebration

For the first anniversary of the Battle of San Jacinto, residents of Houston staged a lavish celebration. A lone star flag on fine silk flew from a huge flagpole in the middle of town. The flag bore a single golden star centered on a dark blue background. Hundreds of native tribe members came to the city to perform a dance around the flag. Later that evening, people from as far as 60 miles (97 km) away were guests at a ball held at the state capitol. After a midnight dinner of venison, turkey, wine, cake, and coffee, the dancing continued until the sun came up.

Leaving Office

On December 10, 1838, Mirabeau Lamar succeeded Houston as president of Texas. Lamar had served as Houston's vice president but had become anti-Houston. As the outgoing president, Houston was invited to speak at Lamar's inauguration. And he did—for three hours! Dressed as George Washington with a powdered wig and knee breeches, Houston spoke of his many achievements in office. Lamar was so overwhelmed by Houston's lengthy speech that he could not deliver his own address and had to have his secretary read it for him.

country as a slave state would skew the delicate balance in Congress. Moving too quickly to annex Texas also might raise suspicions that the country had instigated the Texas Revolution. In March 1837, as one of his last acts as president, Andrew Jackson officially recognized the Republic of Texas as an independent nation. While this act lent legitimacy to the government of Texas, it was not what most Texans had been hoping for, and Houston was disappointed.

Although he did not completely give up on the idea of becoming part of the United States, Houston now knew that Texas would be on its own for the foreseeable future. He set out to stabilize the nation's financial situation and set up its own paper currency. He also sought recognition and trade opportunities with European nations such as France and Great Britain.

Because the Texas Constitution prevented Houston from seeking a second term, he stepped down from office in December 1838. By then, the

Margaret Houston was 26 years younger than her husband.

Texas government, which had rarely had enough money in the treasury to pay Houston his $200 monthly salary, owed him nearly $6,000.

Meeting Margaret Lea

With his official presidential duties at an end, Houston decided to take an extended trip to the United States beginning in May 1839. In part, the trip was to promote Texan land on behalf of the Sabine City Company. This was an enterprise that he had recently helped set up to develop a town at Sabine Pass, near the Gulf of Mexico on the Louisiana border. In Mobile, Alabama, Houston, now in his mid-forties, met Margaret Lea, a quiet, 20-year-old beauty. The two fell quickly in love. Although Houston had to leave Alabama to complete his business, he returned on his way back to Texas. While there, Margaret accepted his marriage proposal.

Her family insisted that the couple wait a proper interval before marrying,

Margaret Lea Houston

Margaret Lea was born on April 11, 1819, in Marion, Alabama, to Temple Lea, a Baptist minister, and his wife, Nancy. As a child, she was shy and suffered from asthma. She was educated at the Judson Institute near her home and loved to read romances by Sir Walter Scott. Throughout her life, Margaret was dedicated to her Christian faith.

At 17, Margaret traveled to New Orleans. She saw Houston when he arrived for treatment of his leg wound after the Texas Revolution. Afterward, she insisted that it was love at first sight. Despite the age difference—she was 20 and he was 46 when they met in Alabama—Margaret fell deeply in love with Houston. As she waited for their wedding day, she wrote a number of poems to her husband-to-be. In one, she described looking at a small portrait of Houston that he had given her:

Dear gentle shade of him I love,
I've gazed upon Thee till thine eye,
in liquid light doth seem to move,
and look on me in sympathy.[1]

so Houston returned to Texas alone. When he arrived, he found that he had been elected to the Texas Congress while he was gone. Once again, Houston took up the cause of the Cherokees. He dedicated much of his energy in Congress to arguing on their behalf, but he met with little success.

In May 1840, Houston returned to Alabama. On May 9, he and Margaret were wed in a ceremony at her brother's house in Marion. Afterward, the newlyweds headed to Texas. Margaret worked to reform Houston. She knew of his reputation as a drunkard. During his years in Texas, he had continued to drink as heavily as in the past, and she was determined to change his ways. Much to the surprise of Houston's longtime friends, she was successful. From the time they arrived in Texas, Houston drank alcohol only for medical purposes.

The Capital

The frontier town of Columbia served as the first capital of the Republic of Texas. After only three months, the capital was moved to the new city of Houston, near the site of the Battle of San Jacinto. The city of Houston quickly gained a reputation as a rough town with a number of saloons, dance halls, and gambling establishments that were open 24 hours a day every day of the year. It also became one of the murder capitals of the state. In 1839, the capital was moved to Waterloo, which was then renamed Austin.

Soon, Houston and his new wife settled into a small, rough home he had built at Cedar Point near Galveston Bay. Houston could not remain there, however. He had to return to Austin, which had recently been made the capital, to attend to his duties in the Texas Congress. Margaret did not accompany her husband, but the two exchanged frequent letters. Houston often professed his loneliness at being far from his wife. In September 1840, he wrote Margaret: "Every hour that we are apart, only resolves me more firmly not again to be separated from you."[2]

*Sam Houston entering the city of Houston in 1837. The newly founded
city was named in his honor after he became Texas's first president.*

The flag of Texas has one star. Texas is sometimes called the "Lone Star State."

LOOKING TO AMERICA

espite his resolve not to be separated from his wife again, Sam Houston soon ran for an office that would keep him away from home even more often. On April 8, 1841, he was nominated to run for Texas president again. After a bitter campaign, Houston was elected in September and soon headed back to Austin. Once again, Margaret did not accompany her husband to the capital.

Houston was sworn in as president on December 13, 1841, before a crowd of more than 1,000 people. As during his first term, he had to determine how to solve the nation's problems without money—the treasury was still empty. Mexico remained a threat. Santa Anna reportedly was preparing to invade Texas. With no money and only a small, poorly disciplined army, Houston was determined to avoid a war.

In March 1842, a Mexican army captured the towns of San Antonio, Refugio, and Goliad; it withdrew less than a week later. Many people in Texas felt that the invasion was the equivalent of a declaration of war and clamored to take up arms.

Stylish Dress

For most of his life, Houston was known to favor flashy clothing. Before the 1841 presidential election had even been held, Houston ordered his inauguration outfit. It was a green velvet suit embroidered in gold. It was topped by a green velvet cape and hat. However, after winning the election, he chose not to wear the showy ensemble. He dressed instead in pantaloons, a hunting shirt, and a fur hat.

Unwanted Visitors

As Houston tried to direct the affairs of his country, he had to make time for its citizens, many of whom felt free to drop in his office at any time. Not everyone came on important business, either. As he complained to a friend, "Some call on business, some through curiosity, and others, as they say 'to spend the time.' Now, this last is cruel to me. If they choose to waste their own time, why that is all right; but they ought to reflect when they are consuming mine that it is of some value to me and to the country."[1]

Wanting to appease his citizens but avoid a drawn-out conflict, Houston ordered each county in Texas to prepare its militia. But he soon ordered the soldiers to stand down. When Mexican troops again invaded in September, Houston ordered the militias to pursue the Mexicans to make sure they left Texas soil, but they were not to pursue them into Mexico. Although the Mexicans withdrew, a number of Texans still followed them into Mexico and were taken as prisoners.

In addition to addressing the Mexican threat, Houston once again sought to restore relations with the American Indian tribes. He urged trade with them as a way to maintain peace and to generate income. As in his first term, Congress was uncooperative. Nonetheless, Houston made efforts at peace. He invited tribe members to visit him in the capital, held council with them, and offered gifts. Due to his efforts, there were few hostilities during this time period.

Starting a Family

In September 1842, Houston moved the capital of Texas from Austin to Houston, and then to Washington-on-the-Brazos. City leaders offered to provide comfortable rooms for government officials. This time, Margaret accompanied her husband to the new seat of government. Margaret was pregnant when they moved, and on May 25, 1843, she gave birth to the couple's first son.

The Archives War

In 1839, after Houston's first term as president, Austin became the capital of Texas. Houston called the city "the most unfortunate site upon earth for the Seat of Government."[3] The new city was far from the republic's other settlements, which made it vulnerable to attack from Mexico. At the beginning of his second presidential term, Houston determined that the Mexican threat to the city was too great. He moved the capital to the city of Houston and later to Washington-on-the-Brazos.

Outraged and determined to retain their city's importance, Austin's citizens decided to hold the government archives hostage. Because the government needed access to its records in order to function, Houston sent representatives to retrieve the papers. Citizens of the town surrounded them and threatened to shoot before the men retreated. Undaunted, Houston sent a larger group of armed men to Austin. They, too, were mobbed and threatened when they tried to remove the archives. Citizens engaged them in a firefight before the men surrendered in order to prevent bloodshed. The city of Austin had won the "Archives War," and in 1844 it became Texas's permanent capital.

At her insistence, they named him
Sam Houston Jr. Soon afterward,
Houston wrote to a friend about his
hopes for the boy: "He is stout, and
I hope will be useful to his kind.
May he be anything but a loafer,
an agitator, or in other words, a
demagogue [manipulative dictator]."[3]

SEEKING STATEHOOD

With efforts at U.S. annexation at
a standstill, Houston spent much of
his second presidential term thinking
about how to bring his country into
the United States. Houston decided
not to press the U.S. government to
accept Texas, which had not worked
in the past. Instead, he took a new
approach and acted indifferent
toward the idea of annexation.
He hinted that if Mexico were to
recognize Texas as a nation, Texas
might ally itself with Great Britain
and remain independent. In April,
the United States and Texas finalized

A Young Namesake

When Sam Houston was
young, he went to great
lengths to differentiate
himself from his father,
Samuel Houston. For
example, he used the
name "Sam" instead of
Samuel, while "com-
pletely rejecting the suffix
'junior,' or 'II.'"[4] Thus when
Sam Houston had his first
son, he named him Sam
Houston Jr. instead of
Samuel Houston III.

an annexation treaty, but there was a problem. The U.S. Senate refused to ratify it because those who opposed slavery feared Texas would become a slave state.

The failure of the treaty sparked wide debate in the United States and became a key issue in that country's presidential campaign of 1844. James Knox Polk, who supported annexation, was elected. Before Polk was sworn into office, however, Houston's term ended.

On December 9, 1844, Houston handed the presidency of Texas over to newly elected Anson Jones. Houston gave Jones some advice. He instructed the new president to keep Texas independent if Great Britain and France were willing to force Mexico to recognize Texas. Houston also urged against annexation if the U.S. Congress did not accept Texas into the union by March 4, 1845. His goal was to spur the United States to action.

As Houston later explained:

If ladies are justified in making use of coquetry [flirtation] in securing their annexation to good and agreeable husbands, you must excuse me for making use of the same means to annex Texas to Uncle Sam. [5]

President James K. Polk believed in annexing Texas, which became a U.S. state during Polk's first year in office.

On February 28, 1845, the U.S. Senate voted to annex Texas. Around the same time, Mexico offered a treaty that pledged to recognize Texas and end all hostilities. Texans now had two choices: join the United States or ratify the Mexican treaty and remain independent. At the end of June, the Texas Congress approved annexation. In October, the issue was brought before Texan voters, who were overwhelmingly in favor of the measure. Texas officially became the twenty-eighth U.S. state on December 29, 1845.

RETIRING TO PRIVATE LIFE?

When Houston left office in December 1844, he had little money. The treasury of Texas was still empty, and he had been paid irregularly and only in small sums. As a result, he now had to earn money by hiring out his slaves, selling his landholdings in Houston, and renting out his home in Cedar Point.

In the spring of 1845, Sam and Margaret took a trip to the United States, where he was greeted as a hero. When they returned home, they settled in a new home near Huntsville. Margaret believed that

Good Company

On the way to Austin for his second presidential term, Houston and his staff stayed overnight at a farm owned by a strong anti-Houston man who had sworn to kill Houston if the two ever met. Unafraid, Houston anonymously spent the evening talking to the farmer's family and leading a Bible study. The next day, the farmer learned Houston's name. He said: "Any man that can talk to my wife and children as you have talked, ask such a blessing on the meals, read the Bible, and comment on it . . . is always welcome to my house."[6] From then on, he was a firm Houston supporter.

A Mistake

Before the Houstons' first child was born, Margaret went to stay with her mother, Nancy, who also had moved to Texas. While Margaret was gone, Houston was offered a bottle of wine as a gift. For the only time during his marriage, he got drunk. Immediately afterward, he rode to his mother-in-law's house to confess to his wife, and she returned home. Her mother, who stayed to help until after the baby was born, accompanied them.

Houston was finally ready to retire to private life. Houston seemed to think so too. He wrote to a friend that he intended to spend his time raising livestock. Houston's life as a farmer would not last long, though. The world of politics continued to call to him.

Sam Houston could only stay away from politics for so long.

Sam Houston erected this home in 1847 in Huntsville, Texas.

SENATOR HOUSTON

lthough Sam Houston seemed determined to retire from politics, in December 1845, he said that he would serve as a U.S. senator if asked to do so. Only two months later, on February 21, 1846, the Texas legislature elected him

to the U.S. Senate, where he would serve for the next
13 years. Margaret was not interested in moving to
Washington DC, however, so the family maintained
its home in Texas. Houston stayed
alone in Washington DC while the
Senate was in session. He arrived
in the capital for his first session of
Congress in March 1846.

Houston had been named
chairman of the Senate's Military
Affairs Committee. When Mexico
declared war on the United States
in April 1846, his input was eagerly
sought. The former Texas president
said that he was in favor of invading
and conquering Mexico. In May,
the United States declared war on
Mexico. When the war ended in
1848, Mexico had lost almost half of
its land.

FIGHTING FOR THE UNION

Houston's biggest concern in the
Senate was the rising hostility over
slavery between the North and South.

U.S. Congress

The U.S. Congress is divided into two chambers, or houses. These are the U.S. Senate and the U.S. House of Representatives. Two senators represent each state in the Senate. The number of representatives for each state is based on its population. Senators serve six-year terms, while representatives serve terms of two years. The two houses work together to pass laws. However, the House of Representatives has the power to begin impeachment proceedings against federal officials; the Senate confirms nominations and approves treaties.

He feared that issue would eventually lead to the breakup of the Union. This prompted him to support the Compromise of 1850. This compromise called for California to join the United States as a free state and for the slave trade to be banned in Washington DC. It also provided a measure that would require Northerners to return runaway slaves to their owners in the South. In supporting the act, Houston's biggest concern was for the Union to remain intact. In a speech to the Senate, he proclaimed:

> *For a nation divided against itself cannot stand. I wish, if this Union must be dissolved, that its ruins may be the monument of my grave, and the graves of my family. I wish no epitaph to be written to tell that I survive the ruin of this glorious Union.*[1]

Houston may have been a slave owner who believed that Southerners

Houston's Religion?

Houston became a Catholic in 1833 in order to gain Mexican citizenship, but he never professed to share the beliefs of the Catholic Church and was not a religious man. However, during his first summer in the U.S. Senate, he began to attend a Baptist church in Washington DC. At home, Margaret often read the Bible to her husband and discussed passages with him. Houston eventually proclaimed that he was a believer, and on November 19, 1854, he was baptized.

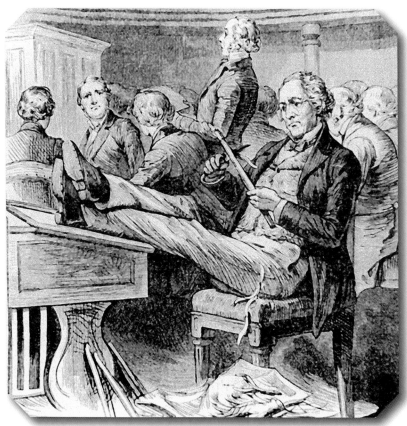

*One of Houston's hobbies was to whittle, or carve wood,
which he sometimes did while in the Senate.*

should remain free to own slaves if they so chose.
Even so, his focus on the Union gained him
popularity in the North and West while earning
him the condemnation of many in the South.
When the compromise was enacted, Houston's
prominence rose.

Eye on the Presidency

With his newfound popularity, Houston received numerous speaking requests. In early 1851, he began a speaking tour in the North. For the most part, his speeches were lighthearted rather than political. They centered on San Jacinto, frontier life, or abstaining from alcohol. His goal at this point was simply to increase his fame—he was considering a run for president in the next year's election.

Despite his rising popularity and the growing expectation that he would run for president, Houston returned home for

---

The Houston Family

During Houston's years in the Senate, Margaret gave birth to six children: Nancy Elizabeth (1846), Margaret Lea (1848), Mary William (1850), Antoinette Power (1852), Andrew Jackson (1854), and William Rogers (1858). His eldest son, Sam Jr., had been born before Houston entered the Senate, and his youngest son, Temple Lea, was born in 1860, after Houston had left the Senate. Because of his governmental duties, Houston was absent for the births of most of his children, though his letters reveal his pleasure at news of their arrival into the world.

Her husband's long absences often left Margaret depressed and melancholy. In 1854, she asked him to resign from the Senate. She later wrote to him:

I believe it is wrong for us to be separated as much as we are, and if we should be [able] to meet, I intend to preach you a perfect sermon on the subject.[2]

Although Houston did not leave politics as Margaret wished, he tried to write home as often as possible, sometimes sending letters almost daily.

Sam Houston often gave lighthearted speeches as he prepared to run for president.

the summer of 1851. He was content to farm and be with his family, which by now had grown to four children. Another four would be born in the years

ahead. He wrote to a friend, "When I am at home
. . . I feel no disposition to return again to scenes of
official conflict."[3] In spite of such claims, Houston
was soon traveling back East continuing his speaking
tour of the states in the North. By the end of 1851,
many Americans considered Houston a leading
contender for the Democratic Party's presidential
nomination. But he never officially announced his
candidacy. By 1852, his support began to wane. He
did not receive the nomination.

An Unpopular Stance

Though he had not been selected for the
presidency, Houston still had important work to
do in the Senate. In early 1854, the controversial
Kansas-Nebraska Act was introduced into Congress.
The bill would have created the territories of Kansas
and Nebraska in the West. It would also have allowed
the government of each territory to decide whether
or not to allow slavery on its land. The bill would
essentially repeal the Missouri Compromise, which
prohibited slavery north of a certain line, known as
the Mason-Dixon Line. For more than 30 years, the
Missouri Compromise had helped to hold the Union
together. The Compromise prevented arguments

over slavery that could have erupted into violence. Houston felt that allowing each state to determine its status would be disastrous for the country.

In a lengthy speech, he predicted that the passage of the Kansas-Nebraska Act would renew the agitation over slavery in the country and cause great problems between the North and South. Despite Houston's speech, the South overwhelmingly supported the Kansas-Nebraska Act. It became law at the end of May. Houston predicted that the result would be war between the North and the South. He told his pastor in Texas, "But, alas! I see my beloved South go down in the unequal contest, in a sea of blood and smoking ruin."[4]

A Biography

As Houston eyed his prospects for the 1852 presidential election, he commissioned Charles Edwards Lester to write his biography. *Sam Houston and His Republic* was published in 1850. In 1855, a revised version appeared as *The Life of Sam Houston*. Since this was a campaign biography, the book was filled with praise for the presidential hopeful.

MISSING ANOTHER CHANCE AT PRESIDENCY

Houston's view was shared by few in the South, where his vote led to increasing unpopularity.

In the North and West, however, Houston's refusal
to support the Kansas-Nebraska Act was heralded,
and his popularity again soared. Soon, "Houston
Clubs" were formed across the North, and people
began to call for Houston to run in the 1856
presidential election. As he had during the 1852
presidential campaign, Houston began to travel
around the North on a speaking tour. Yet, as before,
he never announced his candidacy and was not
chosen to represent any political party on the 1856
ballot.

Houston's term in the U.S. Senate was not due
to expire until 1859. However, in 1857, the Texas
legislature not only announced that it would replace
Houston at the end of his term but also named his
successor two years before the election. At least
two-thirds of the Senate needed to vote in favor
of ousting a Senator. Houston decided that if the
legislature did not want him in the Senate, he would
run for another office—governor of Texas.

Sam Houston, shown in the early 1850s,
was known to be a flashy dresser.

Built in 1856, Texas's Governor's Mansion was once home to Sam Houston. Today, the building is designated a National Historic Landmark.

BACK TO
THE LONE STAR STATE

After announcing his bid for Texas governor in May 1857, the 64-year-old Sam Houston began a grueling campaign tour of his state. In only two months, he traveled more than 1,500 miles (2,414 km) by buggy, spending most nights camped outdoors. At each campaign stop, he delivered a two- or three-hour speech. Although Houston was confident that he would win the election, he received only 27,500 votes to his opponent's 36,257. It was the only election in which he was defeated.

Although he would not be the governor of Texas, Houston was still a U.S. senator for a time. His work in that legislative body was hampered because the election of his successor had made him a lame duck. While few of his fellow senators paid attention to him, Houston began a new tactic to keep the nation together. He tried to rally the country around the idea of making Mexico a protectorate, or territory, of the United States. This was ultimately unsuccessful as few people paid attention to the idea. In March 1859, Houston's term in the Senate ended, and he packed his bags to return home to Texas.

The Governor

Although Houston had intended to retire from politics, he received numerous requests to run for governor once again. In June, he announced that he would honor the people's wish. Instead of the exhaustive campaign tour he had made during the previous election, Houston decided he would let his reputation stand for itself. In July, he delivered his only speech of the campaign in Nacogdoches. He defended himself against the attacks of his opponents and once again spoke of the need to keep the country united.

The election was held at the end of August 1859, and Houston was the clear winner. The family moved into the large governor's mansion in Austin. As governor, Houston once again pursued a policy of peace with the American Indian tribes of Texas. He also continued to emphasize defense of the Texas-Mexico border.

Houston and Slavery

Although he supported the maintenance of the Union, Houston was not against slavery and owned slaves throughout his life. According to Jeff Hamilton, who served as Houston's slave from 1853 to 1863, Houston was a kind master. When Hamilton was 13, Houston bought the young slave to rescue him from being sold to a cruel slave driver. Afterward, Houston treated the boy to candy and a new hat.

Hamilton reported that Houston allowed his slaves to keep any money they earned for work they did outside of the household. They were also taught the basics of reading, writing, and arithmetic. Houston provided good shoes and clothing, and if the slaves fell ill, he made sure they were treated to the best care available.

According to Hamilton, in September 1862, Houston read the Emancipation Proclamation. The orders, which were issued by President Lincoln, declared that slaveholders would be required to free their slaves in January 1863. Several weeks later, Houston announced that if they wished, his slaves could have their freedom before that date. Some historians dispute this account, however, as Houston still owned 12 slaves at the time of his death.

One Last Try for President

Shortly after Houston was elected governor, people across the state began to call for him to run in the 1860 presidential election. A group of supporters in Galveston asked Houston for permission to submit his name as a nominee for the Democratic Convention. But Houston responded that he would not operate within the convention system. He insisted that if he were to be nominated for president, it would have to be by the people and not by a political party.

In response, individuals and newspapers across the country set out to make Houston the "people's candidate." Despite his opposition to the convention system, Houston's name was placed on the ballot at the convention of the Constitutional Union Party in May 1860, but he did not receive the party's nomination.

Afterward, Houston announced that he would answer the calls of the public and run as the people's candidate. He gave several campaign speeches, but by early August it was apparent that he would not be a contender in the election. He withdrew from the race later that month.

In 1852, Houston, second row, fifth from the right, met with other political leaders to try to hold the Union together.

Secession

In November 1860, Abraham Lincoln was elected president of the United States. Soon afterward, one state after another in the South began to secede from the Union. Houston watched in alarm as more and more Texans began to call for secession, too. Margaret noted her husband's fears for the country in a letter to her mother in January 1861: "General Houston seems cheerful and hopeful through the day, but in the still watches of the night I hear him agonizing in prayer for our distracted country."[1]

Confirming Houston's fears, the people of Texas elected a special secession convention, which met on January 28, 1861. The convention voted 166 to 8 in favor of secession. On February 23, voters in a statewide referendum expressed their overwhelming support for secession as well. Despite his desire to remain in the Union, Houston had promised to stand by the will of the people of Texas. Now he attempted to do that. However, he had his own solution—making and keeping Texas independent.

Independence was not what the leaders of the convention had in mind, however. In March, the convention met again. This time they voted to join Texas to the Confederacy—the new country formed by those Southern states that had seceded from the

Sam Jr.

Houston's son Sam Jr. volunteered to join the Texas army and fight for the South in the Civil War. At the Battle of Shiloh in April 1862 in Tennessee, Sam Jr. was shot in the groin and left on the field among the dead. A Union chaplain saw that the young soldier was still alive and recognized the name in the Bible he carried. The chaplain, who knew Sam's father, saw to it that he was cared for. He was taken to Chicago as a prisoner of war, and in September, he was sent back to his family.

The Speech

The night before his refusal to swear his allegiance to the Confederacy, Houston wrote a long speech in which he explained that he was trying to uphold the Texas constitution. He wrote that he knew the consequences of his refusal would likely be removal from office, but he could not go against his conscience, despite the pain it caused him. Although Houston chose not to deliver the speech—he knew it would have no effect on the course Texas would take—he did have it published.

Union. Houston declared this act unconstitutional, but he had little power to stop it. On March 14, delegates to the convention told Houston that he would be required— along with all state officials—to swear an oath of allegiance to the Confederacy. Houston agonized over whether or not to take the oath. After a long night of soul-searching, he told his wife, "Margaret, I will never do it."[2]

He went to his office on March 16. When called by the convention to take the oath, he remained there, whittling. The next day, Houston found that he was no longer governor; because he had refused to take the oath, his lieutenant governor had been given his position.

FINAL YEARS

As Houston had predicted, Southern secession led to civil war. The first shots of the war were fired on April 12, 1861, on Fort Sumter, South Carolina.

Despite his opposition to secession, Houston declared in May that he would support the Confederacy. He would stand by his state and his new country until the South had won its independence.

Houston and his family retired to their home in Cedar Point. He farmed and sold firewood to provide for his family. Money was still an issue as the state owed him a significant amount of back salary. In October 1862, the Union army arrived in nearby Galveston and Houston moved his family away to Huntsville, Texas. He sadly followed the progress of the Civil War and continued to travel the state making speeches. There were even some calls for him to run for governor again, although by now Houston was officially done with politics.

In the summer of 1863 Houston contracted pneumonia, and on July 26, the hero of San Jacinto

Fate of the Family

Houston left his large family with little money when he died. The government still owed him part of his back salary. A number of friends and acquaintances owed Houston money as well. Generous friends helped the family get by, and in 1866, the Texas government finally paid Margaret her late husband's remaining salary, amounting to nearly $2,000. The next year, Margaret contracted yellow fever, and she died on December 3, 1867. Her youngest children went to live with their eldest sister, Nancy Elizabeth.

Recognition

After Houston's death, the same Texas legislature that had given him so much trouble as governor passed a resolution recognizing his contributions to the state. It read in part: "In his death the State has lost one its most distinguished citizens and public servants, and one of its ablest and most zealous advocates, and defenders of its rights, liberties, and its honor."[4]

died. Margaret arranged a small funeral in their home's upstairs parlor, after which Houston was buried in Huntsville's Oakwood Cemetery. Nearly half a century later, a monument was erected above his grave. Inscribed on it is an epitaph attributed to Andrew Jackson: "The world will take care of Houston's fame."[3]

Sam Houston's grave marker is a popular historic site
for visitors to Huntsville, Texas.

TIMELINE

1793	1807	1809
Sam Houston is born on March 2 on the Timber Ridge plantation in Virginia's Shenandoah Valley.	After the death of Houston's father, his family moves to Tennessee in April.	Houston runs away and lives with a group of Cherokees on Hiwassee Island. Oolooteka becomes Houston's adoptive father.

1823	1827	1829
In September, Houston is elected to the U.S. House of Representatives for Tennessee.	Houston is elected governor of Tennessee in August.	On January 22, Houston marries Eliza Allen, who leaves him in April. He resigns as governor and moves to Arkansas Territory.

1813

Houston joins the
U.S. Army in March.

1817

In October, Houston
is appointed as a
government agent
to the Hiwassee
Cherokees.

1818

Houston resigns
from the army and
becomes a lawyer
in Tennessee.

1830

Houston marries
Diana Rogers, a
Cherokee of mixed
descent, during
the summer.

1832

In April and May,
Houston is tried
by the U.S. House
of Representatives
for assaulting
Congressman
William Stanbery.

1836

On March 2,
Houston signs the
Texas Declaration
of Independence.
He is appointed
commander in chief
of Texan forces.

TIMELINE

1836

Houston leads his troops to victory in the Battle of San Jacinto on April 21, ending the Texas Revolution.

1836

Houston is elected president of Texas on September 5 and is inaugurated on October 22.

1839

In the fall, Houston is elected to the Texas Congress.

1854

Houston votes against the Kansas-Nebraska Act. He is praised in the North and West and condemned in the South.

1857

Houston runs for governor of Texas but is defeated on August 3.

1840

Houston marries
Margaret Lea in
Marion, Alabama,
on May 9.

1841

On December 13,
Houston is sworn in
for his second term as
president of Texas.

1846

On February 21,
Houston is elected to
the U.S. Senate for
Texas and serves for
13 years.

1859

Houston is elected
governor of Texas and
is inaugurated
on December 21.

1863

Houston dies
of pneumonia
on July 26.

Essential Facts

Date of Birth

March 2, 1793

Place of Birth

Timber Ridge, Virginia

Date of Death

July 26, 1863

Parents

Samuel and Elizabeth Houston

Marriage

Eliza Allen (January 22, 1829), Diana Rogers (summer 1830), Margaret Lea (May 9, 1840)

Children

Sam Jr., Nancy Elizabeth, Margaret Lea, Mary William, Antoinette Power, Andrew Jackson, William Rogers, Temple Lea

Career Highlights

❖ Houston served in the U.S. Army and was wounded in the Battle of Horseshoe Bend during the War of 1812.
❖ In 1819, Houston was elected solicitor general of Nashville and then served in the U.S. House of Representatives for Tennessee.

❖ In 1827, Houston was elected governor of Tennessee.

❖ During the Texas Revolution in 1836, Houston served as commander in chief of Texan forces.

❖ Houston served twice as president of the Republic of Texas, elected in 1836 and 1841.

❖ After Texas achieved statehood in 1845, Houston was elected to the U.S. Senate and served for 13 years. In 1859, Houston was elected governor of Texas.

SOCIETAL CONTRIBUTION

Beginning in 1836, Houston spent more than a quarter of a century serving the people of Texas. As a young man, he served and was injured in the War of 1812. As a congressman and governor of Tennessee, he worked to bring improvements to that state and to other western lands.

CONFLICTS

Some of Houston's political enemies publicly questioned his role in the Battle of San Jacinto and accused him of cowardice for his long retreat before the battle. When Houston called for national unity before the Civil War, many Southern politicians condemned him. When he refused to swear allegiance to the Confederacy, he was removed from the office of Texas governor.

QUOTE

"For a nation divided against itself cannot stand. I wish, if this Union must be dissolved, that its ruins may be the monument of my grave, and the graves of my family. I wish no epitaph to be written to tell that I survive the ruin of this glorious Union."
—*Sam Houston*

ADDITIONAL RESOURCES

SELECT BIBLIOGRAPHY

Campbell, Randolph B. *Sam Houston and the American Southwest.* New York, NY: Harpers, 1993.

Crane, William Carey. *Life and Select Literary Remains of Sam Houston of Texas.* Freeport, NY: Books for Libraries Press, 1884.

Haley, James L. *Sam Houston.* Norman, OK: University of Oklahoma Press, 2002.

Lester, Charles Edwards. *The Life of Sam Houston: The Only Authentic Memoir of Him Ever Published.* New York, NY: J.C. Derby, 1855.

Williams, Amelia, and Eugene Barker, eds. *The Writings of Sam Houston.* 8 vols. Austin, TX: Pemberton Press, 1970.

FURTHER READING

Caravantes, Peggy. *An American in Texas: The Story of Sam Houston.* Greensboro, NC: Morgan Reynolds Publishing, 2004.

Hatch, Thom. *Encyclopedia of the Alamo and the Texas Revolution.* Jefferson, NC: McFarland, 1999.

Woodward, Walter M. *Sam Houston: For Texas and the Union.* New York, NY: PowerPlus Books, 2003.

Web Links

To learn more about Samuel Houston, visit ABDO Publishing Company online at **www.abdopublishing.com**. Web sites about Samuel Houston are featured on our Book Links page. These links are routinely monitored and updated to provide the most current information available.

Places to Visit

Horseshoe Bend National Military Park
11288 Horseshoe Bend Road, Daviston, AL 36256
256-234-7111
www.nps.gov/hobe/index.htm
Horseshoe Bend National Military Park preserves the site of the Battle of Horseshoe Bend, where Houston fought and was seriously injured during the War of 1812.

Sam Houston Memorial Museum
1402 Nineteenth Street, Huntsville, TX 77340
936-294-1832
www.shsu.edu/~smm_www/index.html
Located on the property of Houston's former home, Woodland, in Huntsville, the museum features information and artifacts from Houston's life.

San Jacinto Battleground State Historic Site
3523 Battleground Road, LaPorte, TX 77571
281-479-2431
www.tpwd.state.tx.us/spdest/findadest/parks/san_jacinto_battleground/
In addition to the historic battleground, visitors can also tour the San Jacinto Monument, a 570-foot (174-m) tower topped by a 34-foot (10-m) high lone star. The monument contains a historical museum as well as an observation deck.

Glossary

annex
To incorporate the territory of one country or state into another country or state.

archive
A collection of historical documents and records.

assimilate
Integrate by adopting the customs and practices of the dominant culture.

bayou
A marshy area that flows into or out of a lake or river.

canister
A metal ball filled with lead or iron shot, which is scattered when the ball is fired from a cannon.

convention
A meeting of a political party to nominate a candidate to represent the party in an election.

delegate
A representative who is selected to act on behalf of the public at a meeting or convention.

effigy
A crude dummy made to represent a person for the purpose of insulting or ridiculing that person.

ensign
Formerly the lowest ranking officer in the U.S. Army.

epitaph
An inscription on a tombstone written to honor the person buried there.

filibuster
A person who enters a foreign country in order to make war without the authorization of his or her country.

frontier
> An area at the farthest limits of settlement; the area beyond is unexplored or undeveloped land.

grapeshot
> A cluster of small iron balls that are fired from a cannon.

lame duck
> A public official who has little political power because the person will soon leave office and a successor has already been selected.

latitude
> Imaginary lines running horizontally around Earth and indicating a distance north or south of the equator that is measured in degrees.

militia
> An army made up of citizens who are called to service only during an emergency.

protectorate
> A relationship in which a weak country is controlled and protected by another, stronger country.

provisional
> Temporary, serving for the time being.

regular
> A soldier in a professional military force as opposed to a civilian serving in the militia.

secede
> Formally withdraw from membership in an organization, alliance, or political entity.

volley
> When many weapons are fired simultaneously.

SOURCE NOTES

Chapter 1. Hero of San Jacinto

1. Marshall de Bruhl. *Sword of San Jacinto: A Life of Sam Houston*. New York, NY: Random House, 1993. xi.

2. David G. McComb. *Texas, a Modern History*. Austin, TX: University of Texas Press, 1989. 44.

3. James L. Haley. *Sam Houston*. Norman, OK: University of Oklahoma Press, 2002. 97.

4. Homer S. Thrall. *A Pictorial History of Texas, from the Earliest Visits of European Adventurers, to A.D. 1879*. St. Louis, MO.: N.D. Thompson & Co., 1879. 567.

5. Charles Edwards Lester. *The Life of Sam Houston: The Only Authentic Memoir of Him Ever Published*. New York, NY: J.C. Derby, 1855. 124.

Chapter 2. Striking Out Early

1. Charles Edwards Lester. *The Life of Sam Houston: The Only Authentic Memoir of Him Ever Published*. New York, NY: J.C. Derby, 1855. 24.

2. Ibid. 18.

Chapter 3. A Young Soldier
1. Charles Edwards Lester. *The Life of Sam Houston: The Only Authentic Memoir of Him Ever Published*. New York, NY: J.C. Derby, 1855. 303.
2. Ibid. 35.

Chapter 4. Political Rise and Fall
1. Charles Edwards Lester. *The Life of Sam Houston: The Only Authentic Memoir of Him Ever Published*. New York, NY: J.C. Derby, 1855. 46–47.
2. Jack Gregory and Rennard Strickland. *Sam Houston with the Cherokees, 1829–1833*. Austin, TX: University of Texas Press, 1967. 58.
3. George W. Paschal. "The Last Years of Sam Houston." *Harper's New Monthly Magazine*. December 1865: 631. 3 May 2009 <http://cdl.library.cornell.edu/cgi-bin/moa/pageviewer?root=%2Fmoa%2Fharp%2Fharp0032%2F&tif=00641.TIF&cite=&coll=moa&frames=1&view=50>.

Source Notes Continued

Chapter 5. Commander in Chief
1. Anna J. Hardwicke Pennybacker. *A New History of Texas for Schools.* Tyler, TX: Pub. for the author, 1888. 122.
2. James L. Haley. *Sam Houston.* Norman, OK: University of Oklahoma Press, 2002. 125.

Chapter 6. President of the Republic
1. John Hoyt Williams. *Sam Houston: A Biography of the Father of Texas.* New York, NY: Simon & Schuster, 1993. 198.
2. James L. Haley. *Sam Houston.* Norman, OK: University of Oklahoma Press, 2002. 220.

Chapter 7. Looking to America
1. James L. Haley. *Sam Houston.* Norman, OK: University of Oklahoma Press, 2002. 267.
2. Ibid. 215.
3. Ibid. 275.
4. John Hoyt Williams. *Sam Houston: A Biography of the Father of Texas.* New York, NY: Simon & Schuster, 1993. 17.
5. James L. Haley. *Sam Houston.* Norman, OK: University of Oklahoma Press, 2002. 290.
6. Ibid. 230.

Chapter 8. Senator Houston

1. James L. Haley. *Sam Houston*. Norman, OK: University of Oklahoma Press, 2002. 305.
2. John Hoyt Williams. *Sam Houston: A Biography of the Father of Texas*. New York, NY: Simon & Schuster, 1993. 299.
3. James L. Haley. *Sam Houston*. Norman, OK: University of Oklahoma Press, 2002. 312.
4. Georgia J. Burleson, comp. *The Life and Writings of Rufus C. Burleson*. Waco, TX: n.p., 1901. 579.

Chapter 9. Back to the Lone Star State

1. John Hoyt Williams. *Sam Houston: A Biography of the Father of Texas*. New York, NY: Simon & Schuster, 1993. 340.
2. James L. Haley. *Sam Houston*. Norman, OK: University of Oklahoma Press, 2002. 390.
3. Ibid. 423.
4. Ibid. 417.

INDEX

ABOUT THE AUTHOR

Valerie Bodden is a freelance author and editor. She has written nearly 100 children's nonfiction books. Her books have received positive reviews from *School Library Journal, Booklist, ForeWord Magazine, Horn Book Guide, VOYA,* and *Library Media Connection.* Bodden lives in Wisconsin with her husband and their two children.

PHOTO CREDITS

Stock Montage/Getty Images, cover, 3, 35, 97; Don Klumpp/ Getty Images, 6; Library of Congress, 11, 26, 30, 76; B. Anthony Stewart/National Geographic/Getty Images, 12; Bob Thomas/ Popperfoto/Getty Images, 15; Cameron Whitman/iStockphoto, 16, 96 (top); Big Stock Photo, 19; Burcin Tuncer/iStockphoto, 21; Sebastian Santa/iStockphoto, 25; Picture History, 36, 90; North Wind Picture Archives, 42, 72; The Sam Houston Memorial Museum, 45, 50, 61, 75, 95, 96 (bottom), 99; Red Line Editorial, 46, 56, 66; Bettmann/Corbis, 55, 65, 79, 98; Hulton Archive/ Stringer/Getty Images, 81; George Eastman House/Getty Images, 85; David Gilder/iStockphoto, 86, 99 (bottom)